Contents

WHY INSTAGRAM?

INSTAGRAM IS MASSIVE

AND IT'S STILL GROWING

If you've been thinking of joining the world of Instagram, whether that's for business or personal enjoyment you're in the right place!

This guide will teach you how to grow your Instagram following, fast, focusing on Instagrams newest features on the platform, specifically IGTV!

IGTV is one of the best ways to grow your following fast and get tons of new eyes on your page!

WHERE SHOULD YOUR FOCUS BE ON INSTAGRAM?

Most recently, engagement on videos has majorly grown on Instagram. This growth is so significant that the highest amount of engagement is now found on videos compared to regular posts. This is all likely due to the addition of Instagrams hot feature IGTV and the fact you now have the ability to show 'previews' of your IGTV in the newsfeed.

Instagram (and any other social media platform for that matter) will always favour people that use their newest latest features, meaning your content will receive more visibility. It will reach more of your current followers and it may reach the explore feed, so people that don't follow you yet, get the chance to see you.

So if Video is what's hot right now, let's not forget about IG Live and Stories!

If you want more followers, start using Video and get familiar with IGTV, going Live and using Stories..

THE ANSWER: VIDEO (IG LIVE, IGTV & STORIES)

LET'S DIVE IN

How To Create Simple IGTV Content That Grows Your Following Fast

1. PREPARE

What you're looking to do here is create good content that your followers (and new followers) are going to want to consume. Going LIVE on Instagram for the sake of going Live with no real preparation or ideas behind it, is simply a waste of time.

Always think quality quality quality.

Look to deliver content that is of value to your follower. The aim is for you to teach them something, provide entertainment, provide them with some education.

By the end of consuming your content, your follower needs to feel they've learnt something.

This is what is meant by providing 'value' in your content.

Pro Tip : If you're ever unsure of what you should post, or what subject you should talk about in your niche, go and follow some of the top influencers in that niche. I'm sure you are already! Study what they are doing, how they are doing it and the subjects they are talking about. This should give you a big clue as to what you should be doing.

Now that doesn't mean you copy them! You model them. You make it your own based on what you see them doing.

Begin by writing down a few ideas and bullet points that you want to cover. Try and be as brief and direct to the point as possible. Videos between 3-5 do the best on IGTV and Instagram Live. If you like to waffle, and go off topic, being prepared with your notes will help you cut down on time!

Don't forget a "call to action" at the end of your video which will tell people what to do next (i.e comment below, click the link, send me a DM, sign up here, click add to cart).

Whatever your call to action may be, this is super important! If you are delivering good value content in your IGTV and Insta Lives people will stick around and watch, take advantage of the fact you have their attention and get them to take the next step with you.

This is going to build your brand, get you more followers and if you have a business allow people to take the next step with you.

2. How To Turn Instagram Stories Into IGTV Content!

This is the ultimate hack right here! Record continuously using the Instagram story " FOCUS " feature with headroom.

Open Instagram Stories and record a continuous video using Instagram's "Focus" feature. (Tip, the Focus feature does tend to move about quite a bit on the Instagram interface, you may need to play around a bit to find this feature). Currently Instagram allows you to record an Instagram Story for up to 2 minutes at a time (however this does change). Hold down on the record button the entire time you film your content OR use a bluetooth device so you can go hands free.

By the way, it's important to note here, you do not need any fancy software to do this, you are simply using your phone and the Instagram app!

You don't even need any special lighting equipment with the Focus feature. I love this feature as I simply grab my phone and deliver my content.

It's one less hurdle.

Instagram will automatically crop your video squared when displaying the preview in the newsfeed. It's important when you shoot your first minute leave some "headroom" or extra space above your head and face.

This will allow for some nice cropping. I.e when your "preview" shows up in the newsfeed you haven't chopped your face in half!

Here's an example of the Focus feature.

I love using it because it makes my content look more professional and I haven't had to use any lighting equipment.

I also love to use the Focus feature to take selfies and create covers, but more on that shortly.

3. Now Save Each Clip You Record In Order

Once you've finished filming, instead of hitting "post" save each individual clip to your camera roll in order!

When you're recording, every 15 seconds, an individual singular clip will appear at the bottom of your screen (see the example below). You can save each clip as you go or tap each individual clip and then save it to your phone in the order you recorded it (super important). Do this for each individual clip.

Pro Tip : You can also hit "post" AFTER saving your individual clips and have your content show up in your stories. Stories are HOT right now and they're not going away anytime soon. Make the most of the content you just created and share this to your stories at the same.

4. Time To Pick Up Where You Left Off

- Unless you were finished with your content, open Instagram Stories again, chose the "Focus" feature again and begin recording.
- Pick up right where you left off. You can record another 2 x minutes worth (8 individual clips).
- Keep repeating until you're finished, bearing in mind that IGTV only allows you up to 10 minutes! And 3-5 minute videos are what perform best.
- Once you've finished don't forget your call to action to maximise your efforts.

Pro Tip: The quality of your content is always more important than the length. If you are delivering great content, whether that be educational, entertaining or thought provoking people will stick around. Remember to model successful influencers in your niche.

Pro Tip: Again if you are struggling to think of content you should talk about ask your followers what they'd like to see! There is nothing more powerful than asking your existing following what content they'd like you to create or what they already enjoy about following you.

5. Import Video Clips Into A Video Editing App

Personally I love to use InShot. Open the app, then import the individual video clips from your camera roll into the app in the order your recorded them (super important). To make this easier, they must be saved in the right order to begin with!

Some other photo and video editing apps you can use! For this tutorial I'm using InShot, but here's a list of others to check out as well:

- Vont
- Videorama
- PicPlayPost
- iMovie
- Clips
- Clipomatic
- CutStory
- Add Subtitles

6. Review & Export Your Video

Go over the finished video, edit and review your complete video making sure you've pasted the clips in the right order. Otherwise your video won't make much sense. You can also add intro music, add transitions add text overlays and add other fancy effects, if you want to.

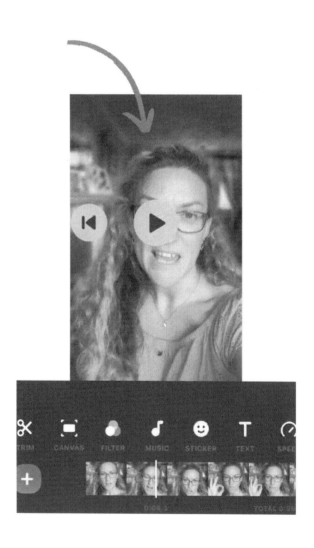

7. Create A Cover Photo Thumbnail For Your Finished Video That You Will Upload To IGTV

Open up Instagram Stories again, this time selecting the Focus lens and take a selfie with either your face or the subject matter in the centre of the screen. Remember to leave some space in the top 1/4 of the screen for cropping.

This will ensure that the thumbnail will fit nicely when it's cropped into a square for the Instagram feed. Save that photo to your camera roll.

Pro Tip : Upload that photo to a font app like 'Over' to add title text.

Keep in mind that Instagram will crop your thumbnail squared, so be mindful of this when adding your text overlay.

Once you've created your thumbnail, export it to your camera roll ready to add it to your brand new IGTV video!

8. Upload Your Video To IGTV (#Boom)

Tap the IGTV icon in your feed or you can do this under your bio section and upload your new full length video! You'll also have the option to select the thumbnail you created from your camera roll. You will then create a title for this video and it will appear as the first comment under the preview on your main page.

Pro Tip: As your title, use a question that will get people to take action!

Then use 3 very specific qualified hashtags that relate to the topic of your video to help your IGTV video get discovered! (More on hashtags shortly)

14

9. Select Post Preview and Make Visible To Facebook

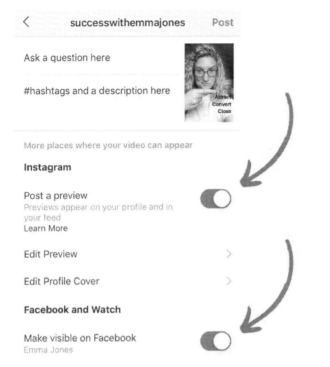

Select 'Post a preview' to allow the first minute of your IGTV video to appear in the news feed, explore page and your grid on your profile!

This will entice people to jump over and watch your IGTV!

Select 'Make visible on Facebook' and bam, you've instantly repurposed your content and are reaching a new audience with the push of a button.

Hit POST and voila, you're done!

10. Share Your IGTV To Your Instagram Story

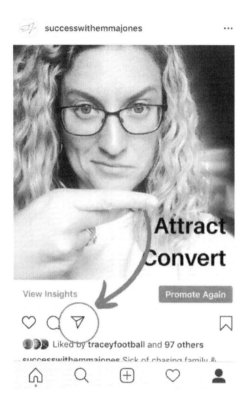

We're not done yet!

Share your IGTV video to your Stories whilst using a relevant hashtag (more training to follow in the hashtag section) to get your IGTV out in front of a brand new audience AND giving great content to your existing followers.

Click the icon above to share your IGTV to your Story.

Pro Tip : This one tactic can help your IGTV viewers double, and more importantly this can also help you get more followers, which is what you want right?

BONUS PRO TIP

Repurpose Your IGTV Video Onto Other Platforms!

If you want to really get the most out of your new IGTV video you just created and want to build you brand even more share onto other platforms!

Don't just leave it sitting on your camera roll...

Did you know YouTube has recently allowed you to now post vertical videos? Previously all videos uploaded had to be displayed horizontally. This is GREAT news if you have other platforms and want to build your brand. Now, you can share that IGTV, repurpose it onto YouTube and any other platform you choose!

I share mine onto YouTube, Facebook, My group on Facebook, with my email list and even onto Linkedin.

IGTV TIPS & HACKS

- **Consistency is king.** As with anything the key to success with IGTV is consistency. You can't expect to post one IGTV and have a ton of followers. You have to be consistent. Think of your IGTV channel like your own show.

- **Post on the same day and same time if possible.** Your audience will get used to when you post and will actively look for your content.

- **Add previews and promote your videos.** Always choose to add a preview to the newsfeed and your profile page so you can increase your views and get more followers.

- **Share your IGTV to your Story.** Again this could double your chance of getting new followers. Stories are HOT on Instagram

- **Answer questions from your followers.** Create a poll in your Stories asking your audience a question on what IGTV they would like you to create. Ask your audience questions, collect the questions and make short videos answering what they want to know. This is the easiest hack for creating IGTV videos and giving your followers what they want.

- **Reply to comments on your videos quickly.** Instagram favours IGTV's and any content for that matter that shows more engagement.

- **Check out your analytics to see what's working and check your insights.** After publishing your IGTV you can click the button with the three dots and "View Insights". Checking these will tell you what your audience is responding to, the topics you're covering, the IGTV length, type of video, titles descriptions, hashtags etc. This will give you another clue as to what IGTV's you should continue to create for your followers.

THE LATEST HASHTAG HACKS

Did you know that the most recent studies show that using more hashtags can actually hurt your engagement!

Previously it was recommended that you use up to 30 hashtags and up to 10 in your Story, what works better is 5 hashtags or less in your posts and 1 on your Story!

Make sure these hashtags are really targeted and relevant to your content!

Pro Tip : Less is more! Relevant hashtags win!

LESS IS MORE!

Remember just having hashtags won't grow your followers like it used to on Instagram!

You MUST have quality content. If your content is good and makes people engage and stick around this is what is KEY. Hashtags will help and you must *always* use them, but quality is key here.

The hashtags you want to use will depend on what niche and space your business or personal account operates in.

How To Find Relevant Hashtags To Use For Your Content

Do a little hashtag research in your niche to see what people are searching for.

Let's look at weight loss for example

1.Head to the 'Explore' feature within Instagram

2.Type into the 'search' bar at the top a topic from your niche. In this example we're looking at weight loss

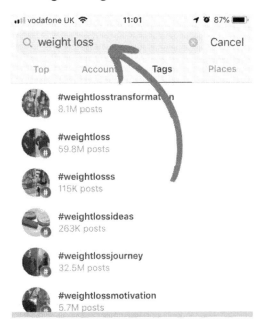

Notice all the different hashtags that pop up here that you can use!

Use this as inspiration and ideas to find relevant hashtags for your niche.

Pro Tip : Stay away from hashtags that have millions of posts! Try to drill down to find hashtags that don't have as much competition but are still relevant. This is specific to *posts in the newsfeed* (not stories but we'll cover that in the stories section)

This means when you use those hashtags your content has more chance of being seen.

If you use hashtags that are very popular and have millions of posts you run the risk of YOUR amazing content getting buried in the explore feed.

3.Now let's go one step further and drill down more into these hashtags to find more examples with less competition and grab more ideas.

Click on one of the hashtags and another page will pop up with more ideas AND ideas for posts!

Pro Tip : By doing this you should ALWAYS find inspiration for post ideas as well as hashtags.

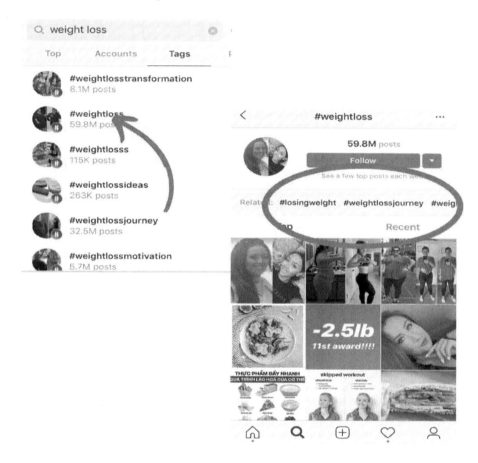

Here's another example : Beauty.

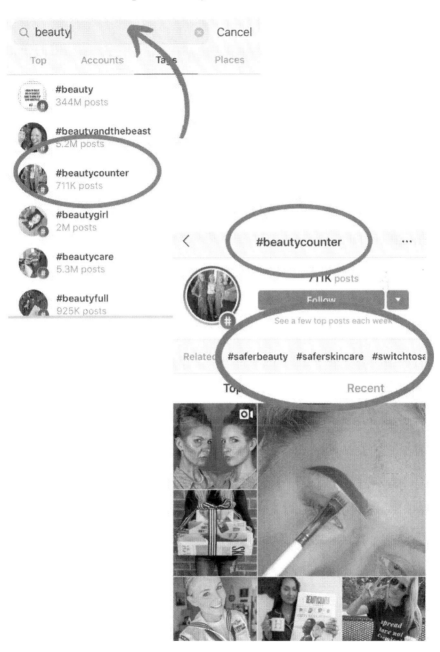

4.Upload your post / IGTV and simply add your hashtags in the comments.

Remember, use hashtags with less competition.

ALWAYS use hashtags, this is what will help you get more followers. It allows people to find YOU.

Test out different hashtags, and study your insights to see which hashtags work the best for you.

CREATE BRANDED HASHTAGS

Consider creating a "branded" hashtag that's relevant and unique to you and your brand/business. For example, I use the hashtag #SuccessWithEmmaJones or #successwithemmajones. Now it doesn't have to be your company or account name it can be branded to your message, your products, something unique to you. Using it on your posts builds your hashtag following and it allows your followers to use the hashtag also. Connect with your fans on a deeper level

PRO TIP:

USE HASHTAGS WITH LESS COMPETITION

This is something I have been testing with great results! Don't go after the hashtags with millions of posts, as mentioned above you run the risk of your brilliant content getting lost to competitors with many more followers than you.

When choosing hashtags (for your posts not stories! More on that in the stories section) go after the less competitive ones, with less posts. See the screen shot below. #mindset has 18.6 million posts, where as #mindsets has 112k posts.

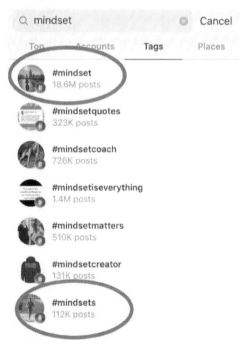

INSTAGRAM STORIES:

CREATE DEEPER CONNECTIONS AND GROW YOUR FOLLOWING

Most people now say that they're spending more and more time looking at stories over page content. Just like IGTV, Stories are super important if you want to grow your following. People like real, authentic and genuine content, and the typical post in the feed isn't this.

Stories are real, and real makes people feel good. People want to know who you really are, now for some they don't want to share every aspect of their life and that's ok. You don't have to flood your Stories with every moment and experience you have throughout your day, but do let them see the real you from time to time.

People can't get to know the real you from a magazine-like feed.

This is what you're aiming for here. To share more real genuine content sharing your daily life to create deeper connections with your existing following and draw new followers in.

Before followers choose to hit the 'follow' button, don't forget they're browsing around your profile first. They're more likely to go to your Stories first. Bare that in mind.

PRO TIP :

MODEL SUCCESSFUL IG ACCOUNTS

If you're unsure what type of content you should be sharing in your stories, or what type of stories get the most engagement, one of my biggest tips and advice is to go and follow an influencer in your niche.

Follow an account that has a huge following. What are the big pages doing?

If you want to achieve something that others have, all you have to do is model what they do. This applies to so many aspects of life not just to getting more followers on Instagram!

When I first started building my business online, I studied what other successful people in my niche were doing. What were they doing and how were they doing it.

Now modelling doesn't mean copying! You have to be unique and be able to stand out from the crowd.

It's about finding what's working and making it your own. Don't become a carbon copy of someone else's Instagram account.

If you're unsure how to find top IG accounts in your niche, again use the explore button (the magnifying glass) and type in a search term to come across popular posts and IG accounts.

QUICK TIPS TO USE STORIES TO GROW YOUR FOLLOWING (AND ENGAGE YOUR EXISTING ONE)

1. Add hashtag stickers to your story

You can add hashtag stickers to your story by tapping the hashtag sticker icon. *Now with Stories you want to use BROADER hashtags,* more popular ones, (unlike less popular ones on your posts). This is a strategy I use all the time on my stories to gain new followers. It helps my stories enter the 'explore' feed and for potential new followers to see my content!

As you can see here with an IGTV I shared to my story, I added the hashtag #socialmediamarketing

This allowed my story to be seen by an extra 32 people relatively quick. This means my story came up under that hashtag and allowed new people to watch it.

This is all organic, free viewers too! No pay to play here! All free methods.

Out of the 68 people who had viewed this story, 32 of them were new. This is how you deliver valuable content to your existing followers and attract potential new ones at the same time.

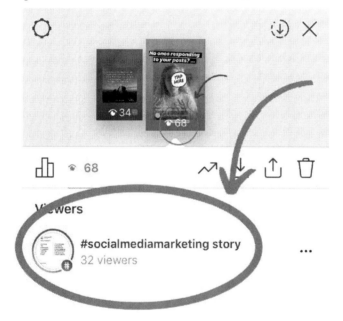

To access this information. Simply click onto your story and click the number underneath your story to grab the insights.

IMPORTANT TIP : For your hashtag to work your profile must be set to Public

LET'S BREAK THIS DOWN....

1. Research Hashtags

- Find the right hashtag to use.
- Make sure it fits well with your story, is it relevant?
- Select a hashtag with a larger volume, for example #weightloss will do better than #weightlosstips
- Unlike with regular posts for the newsfeed you want to use *broader* hashtags for stories
- Use the explore icon below to research hashtags

2. Create Your Story

- The most important aspect about your story is to make it engaging
- Photos will work, however as mentioned previously any type of video, IG Live, IGTV or video clip is what is performing best.
- Focus on *quality* over quantity
- If you need ideas or inspiration try the modelling method. Go find and follow someone who is doing really well on Instagram and study and model what they do. Most importantly making it your own

3. Add Your Hashtag To Your Story

You can lay the hashtag across the photo or video, you can hide it at the bottom or place it where you like.

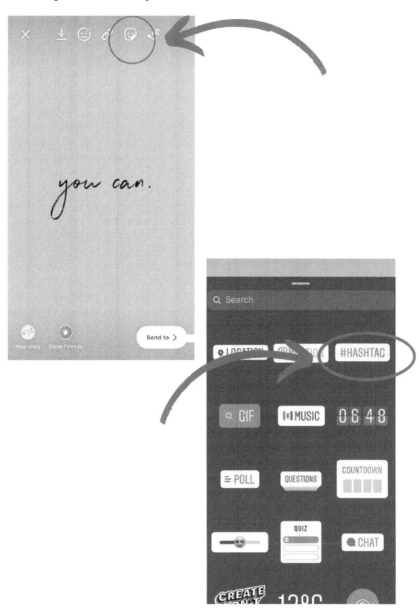

4. Add to your story

5. Adjust As Necessary

If you're not generating extra viewers and followers from your stories then consider changing two things:

Your Content

If your content isn't engaging, people will just swipe past. Again model what's working for others

Your Hashtags (#)

Remember to keep your hashtags broad on stories but also relevant. Switch it up and see which hashtags get you more viewers and followers.

CONCLUSION

Instagram is an amazing platform if you know what to do!

The most important thing you can do is take action with what you've learnt in this guide and be *consistent.*

Nothing in business, or life for that matter, comes easy.

So posting one post or one IGTV and expecting to get a ton of followers from that one post isn't realistic.

Once you become more consistent on Instagram, just like most platforms, the algorythm will start to work in your favour.

Consistency really is king.

And the more you keep taking action from this guide your engagement and followers will increase.

Always take advantage of the newest features that Instagram releases. When Instagram releases something new, say IGTV for example, this is your chance to get the most followers and engagement, as Instagram will be testing the feature and want it to succeed! So that feature will be featured the most on the platform! This is an important rule to remember.

By following the tips in this guide consistently you'll be on the road to a successful Instagram account with growing followers in no time.

LET'S CONNECT!

Share your results with me by using the
hashtag #successwithemmajones
I'd love to see your posts!

Instagram :

https://instagram.com/successwithemmajones/

Facebook :

https://facebook.com/successwithemmajones

Website :

https://www.successwithemmajones.com

Ready to take your business to the next level?

And want FREE training from yours truly?

Learn the secrets of attracting endless customers and business builders?

Then be sure to check out this FREE Attraction Marketing training.

In this 10 day Online Recruiting Bootcamp, you'll learn...

- About how to use the internet to generate leads, separate your hot prospects from the "suspects" and get paid to do it.
- How to become the hunted, instead of the hunter and have prospects knocking down your door or calling you with credit card in hand, ready to join or buy from your business.
- Get a Cool Method to Get Leads & Prospects to Call YOU about Your Business.

Simply visit my website at www.SuccessWithEmmaJones.com

Click on the 'Products' tab

Click on the 'Get Access Now' button, it's free.

If you enjoyed this book...

Please share your thoughts in a REVIEW. Your feedback is really helpful and I would love to hear from you!

Just head back to Amazon to leave a quick review.

Many Thanks

To Your Success!

Emma

Printed in Great Britain
by Amazon

49821625R00024